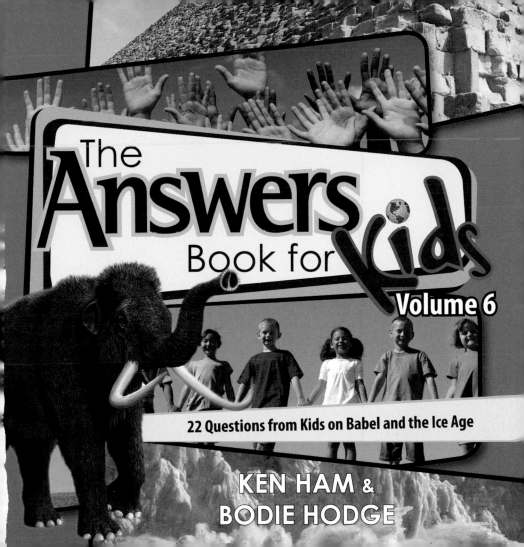

The Answers Book for Kids

Volume 6

22 Questions from Kids on Babel and the Ice Age

KEN HAM & BODIE HODGE

Second Printing: June 2014

Master Books®
P.O. Box 726
Green Forest, AR 72638

Master Books® is a division of the New Leaf Publishing Group, Inc.

Printed in China

Book design by Terry White

ISBN 13: 978-0-89051-783-3
Library of Congress Control Number: 2008904921

All Scripture references are New King James Version unless otherwise noted.

Please visit our website for other great titles: www.masterbooks.net

Special thanks to the kids who contributed from around the world, as well as the kids from Cornerstone Classical Christian Academy for their submissions!

When you see this icon, there will be related Scripture references noted for parents to use in answering their children's, and even their own, questions.

Dear Kids

We hope this book will help answer some of your questions about the Ice Age and the Tower of Babel. We pray that you understand that the Bible is true and that it does explain the world that we live in.

We see a lot of sad things happening in our world, and we all do bad things, too. This is because of sin. When Adam, our mutual grandfather (6,000 years ago), sinned against God and ruined the perfect world God originally created, death and suffering entered the world — so we suffer and die as well because of sin.

But God provided a means to save us from sin and death. He sent His Son Jesus into the world to become a man, live a sinless life, and die on our behalf. He died on a Cross, but He was also resurrected (brought back to life). If we repent (turn from our sin) and believe in Jesus Christ as our Lord and Savior and in His Resurrection, we too will be saved and will spend all eternity with God in heaven with all of His goodness. Please read these Scriptures in this order:

Genesis 1:1, 1:31, 3:17–19; Romans 5:12, 3:23, 6:23, 10:9, 5:1

God bless you.
Ken and Bodie

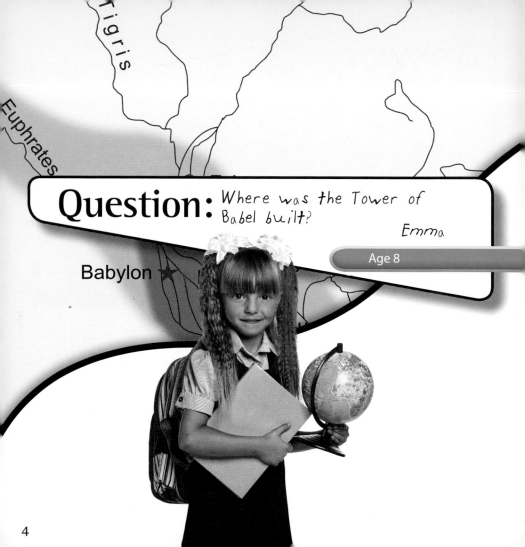

Question: Where was the Tower of Babel built?

Emma

Age 8

Babylon ★

4

Answer:

And it came to pass, as they journeyed from the east, that they found a plain in the land of Shinar, and they dwelt there (Genesis 11:2).

The tower was built at Babel. This was where Noah's descendants settled after they left Noah's home (where he had become a farmer). They traveled from the east and arrived at a place that they called Shinar (shee-NAR), which means "between two rivers."

These two rivers were the Tigris and Euphrates. These rivers formed as a result of Noah's Flood, and were likely named for two pre-Flood rivers that were mentioned in Genesis 2:14. This re-using of familiar names has happened many times down through the ages. For instance, when the Europeans came to the Americas they named rivers, cities, and regions after places in Europe.

Noah's descendants found a plain between these rivers and dwelt there. That plain is where Babel was located. This small city of Babel and the region of Babylonia (the region was later named after the city of Babel) were in southern Mesopotamia, which is part of modern-day Iraq. Later, the city of Babel (or Babylon) became the same site where a big empire was based — the Babylonian Empire, led by Nebuchadnezzar.

The city of Babel was located along the Euphrates River in the plain of Shinar, south of the modern city of Baghdad in Iraq.

2 Kings 20:14; Daniel 11:1

Question:
How big was the Tower of Babel?

Gershom

Answer:

And they said, "Come, let us build ourselves a city, and a tower whose top is in the heavens; let us make a name for ourselves, lest we be scattered abroad over the face of the whole earth" (Genesis 11:4).

The Bible doesn't tell us how big the Tower of Babel was. It is described as "a tower whose top is in the heavens" (Genesis 11:4). This means that it was much taller than the buildings of the city that Noah's descendants were constructing. The tower would have been above them, but it would not have needed to be as big as a skyscraper today. Later, other towers were built in the same area that had names similar to "tower whose top is in the heavens", but these towers were not that big. They were just the largest structures compared to what was around them.

Many believe that the Etemenanki (EH-tuh-meh-NAHN-kee) tower was simply another later name for the Tower of Babel. Etemenanki means "temple of the foundation of heaven and earth." The tower was old and run down by the time of Daniel and Nebuchadnezzar (500–600 B.C.) and Alexander the Great tore it down about 325 B.C.

Judging by the square base where the tower originally was located, an old description on a tablet, and the writing of a historian named Herodotus, the tower was probably about 7–8 stories and 300 feet (91 meters) high. That would definitely be big enough to stand out in a little city!

Genesis 11:3–4; Judges 9:51;
Proverbs 18:10

Question:

How long did it take to build the Tower of Babel?

Eva

Age 8

Answer:

Then they said to one another, "Come, let us make bricks and bake them thoroughly." They had brick for stone, and they had asphalt for mortar (Genesis 11:3).

The Bible doesn't tell us how long it took to build the Tower of Babel, but when people are dedicated to doing something and are working toward the same goal, they can do things very quickly.

For example, Richard the Lionheart, who was king of England in the Middle Ages, had his soldiers build a castle for him in Normandy (a part of France that he ruled). It needed to be built quickly so he could use it. This huge and incredible castle was built in about one year! The ruins of this castle (Chateau Gaillard) still stand today, and they are still very impressive.

A tower would be much easier to build than a complicated castle. A Jewish historian named Josephus, who lived about 2,000 years ago, said of the Tower of Babel, "It grew very high, sooner than anyone could expect."

The people who built the Tower of Babel in Genesis 11:3–6 were dedicated to the cause of building the tower. It may have been built very quickly, possibly in just a few months — but we don't know for sure.

Genesis 11:3-6

9

Question: How many people did it take to build the Tower?

Laura

Age 8

Answer:

These were the families of the sons of Noah, according to their generations, in their nations; and from these the nations were divided on the earth after the flood (Genesis 10:32).

The Bible in Genesis 10 gives a list of families that came out of Babel with new languages. Since we don't know how many people were in each family, we can't know the exact number of people who came out of Babel. If we add up the families, there were at least 78. There could have been a few more, since the line that goes from Noah to Peleg (ultimately the line of Jesus) doesn't give us all the information. For example, this line contains Noah, Shem, Arphaxad, Selah, Eber, and Peleg. (Some of these sound like strange names, huh?)

But Genesis 11:13 says that Arphaxad had other children. Genesis 11:14 says that Selah had other children. And Genesis 11:17 says that Eber had other children as well. So these families that were not listed specifically in Genesis 10, but mentioned in Genesis 11, may have had a new language and would add to those 78 families. If each of these 78 families had a dad, a mom, and three kids, that would be just under 400 people! One person named Joktan had 13 kids (Genesis 10:26–29). So some families may have had much more than just three children.

Genesis 9:1; Genesis 11:4

11

Question:

What time period was the Tower of Babel built in?

Noah

Age 9

Big Picture of World History

Columbus rediscovers America	A.D. 1496
Normans conquer England	A.D. 1066
Rome loses power to Constantinople	A.D. 324
Jerusalem and the Temple are destroyed	A.D. 70
Christ was born	4 B.C.
Last book of the Old Testament (Malachi)	416 B.C.
Time of the Kings (Saul was first)	1095 B.C.
Time of the Judges (Moses was first)	1491 B.C.
Call of Abraham	1922 B.C.
Tower of Babel	2242 B.C.
Global Flood	2348 B.C.
Curse	4004 B.C.
Creation	4004 B.C.

Answer:

Now this is the genealogy of the sons of Noah: Shem, Ham, and Japheth. And sons were born to them after the flood (Genesis 10:1).

The Tower of Babel incident occurred around 4,200 years ago — about 100 years after the Flood but before Abraham was born, This was before ancient Egypt, Greece, and other early civilizations. These places couldn't have begun until after people left Babel to establish these other civilizations.

Noah's grandson Javan founded Greece. When we read "Greece" in the Old Testament, it is actually the name Javan, which we translate as "Greece." Noah's grandson Mizraim founded Egypt. When we read "Egypt" in the Old Testament, it is the name Mizraim that we translate as "Egypt." Famous and ancient civilizations you are familiar with couldn't have existed until after Babel. This means the Tower of Babel was built prior to the appearance of these ancient cultures.

Genesis 10:32; Genesis 12:10;
Galatians 3:28

Question: Is the Tower of Babel still here?

Paige

Age 9

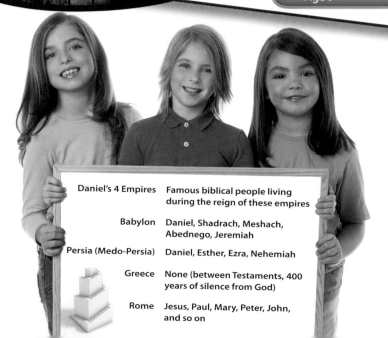

Daniel's 4 Empires	Famous biblical people living during the reign of these empires
Babylon	Daniel, Shadrach, Meshach, Abednego, Jeremiah
Persia (Medo-Persia)	Daniel, Esther, Ezra, Nehemiah
Greece	None (between Testaments, 400 years of silence from God)
Rome	Jesus, Paul, Mary, Peter, John, and so on

Answer:

So the LORD scattered them abroad from there over the face of all the earth, and they ceased building the city (Genesis 11:8).

The Tower of Babel is not around anymore. If it were, it would be over 4,200 years old. There are not too many things that can last that long, even if they are made from baked bricks!

The Tower of Babel was said to be an old run-down building over 2,500 years ago. The ruler of the Babylonian Empire, Nebuchadnezzar, wanted to tear it down and rebuild it. But he didn't get an opportunity to. He said:

"Since a remote time, people had abandoned it, without order expressing their words. Since that time earthquakes and lightning had dispersed its sun-dried clay; the bricks of the casing had split, and the earth of the interior had been scattered in heaps."

After the Babylonian Empire, other empires came to power. Daniel, who lived during the same time as Nebuchadnezzar (and lived into the Persian Empire), prophesied about these kingdoms in Daniel 2.

Alexander the Great, who was the founder of the third empire (Greece), did tear down the Tower of Babel. He also wanted to rebuild it. But Alexander died at a very young age, before he could rebuild it, so the tower passed into history.

*Job 3:14; Daniel 3:28;
Daniel 4:27*

HOLY BIBLE

15

Question:
Are there any archaeological remains of the Tower of Babel?

Becca and Brianna

Age 9 & 7

Answer:

With kings and counselors of the earth, who built ruins for themselves (Job 3:14).

There really isn't much left of the Tower of Babel. Alexander the Great removed bricks and the outer coating, but he never rebuilt it. However, most researchers think they know where the foundation is located.

Also, there was an archaeological artifact found called a "stele." A stele (pronounced the same as steal or steel) is actually a rock slab with pictures and inscriptions on it. Archaeologists love finding things like this.

The Tower of Babel stele has an image of Nebuchadnezzar next to the Tower of Babel. It shows its shape as a ziggurat (imagine a step pyramid or a pyramid with several flat layers on it).

About 440 B.C., a historian named Herodotus claimed he saw the tower and described it:

"It has a solid central tower, one furlong square, with a second erected on top of it and then a third, and so on up to eight. All eight towers can be climbed by a spiral way running around the outside, and about halfway up there are seats for those who make the journey to rest on."

This is a great confirmation of the Bible's truthfulness about the Tower of Babel. But remember, the ultimate reason we can know the Tower of Babel existed is because God's Word is true!

2 Kings 19:25

Question: Was there anything inside the Tower of Babel?

Sophia

Age 8

Answer:

And they said, "Come, let us build ourselves a city, and a tower whose top is in the heavens..." (Genesis 11:4).

As far as we know, there was nothing inside the tower. It makes more sense that it would have been solid bricks inside, just like a ziggurat tower you might build of stacked wooden blocks.

But the Tower of Babel did have various level areas on various stories. In the last question, we read that a historian named Herodotus (who had said he had seen the old tower before it was torn down) said that there were seats about halfway up for people to rest.

On the very top of the Tower was the special place. It likely held a little structure as the top or "head" of the Tower. This was long gone by Nebuchadnezzar's day (over 1,500 years later!). He wrote that the head was not "complete."

But Jewish sources called the "Midrash" say the top had been burned. This makes sense because Nebuchadnezzar pointed out that lighting and earthquakes had done damage to the tower. Lighting usually strikes the tallest structure in the area and often starts fires. So if that top structure was struck by lightning, it makes sense that it could have burned and was long gone 1,500 years later when Nebuchadnezzar mentioned it.

Job 15:28; Judges 9:52;
Acts 7:49

Question: Why was Babel made?

Caleb

Age 5

20

Answer:

. . . let us make a name for ourselves, lest we be scattered abroad over the face of the whole earth" (Genesis 11:4).

The tower and city that the people built at Babel were made because they were disobeying what God had told them to do — to move over the earth. They were sinning against God — and possibly going so far as to worship the heavens instead of God.

In Genesis 9:1, God told Noah and his family something very important. Noah's family came off the ark into the new world and God said, "Be fruitful and multiply, and fill the earth."

God repeated this just a few moments later in Genesis 9:7. God said, "And as for you, be fruitful and multiply; bring forth abundantly in the earth and multiply in it."

This was important because there was no one in the world except them. God wanted them to fill the earth and take possession of it, but Noah's descendants decided to disobey God. Instead, they built a city and tower so that they would not be scattered across the earth. We read about this in Genesis 11:4.

God was very patient with them. But finally He confused their language to force them to spread out over the earth (Genesis 11:7–8). This should be a reminder to us — we should always listen to what God says in His Word, the Bible.

Genesis 9:1; Genesis 11:4; Genesis 1:7–8

Question: If everyone would have scattered like God said, would there still be one language?

Neva

Age 8

22

Answer:

Therefore its name is called Babel, because there the LORD confused the language of all the earth; and from there the LORD scattered them abroad over the face of all the earth (Genesis 11:9).

Yes! There was originally only one language, so if everyone had scattered over the earth, they would have continued to speak that language. It is possible that we would have various dialects as people lived in different parts of the world — we even see that today with Canadian English, Australian English, American English, and so on. God created one language when He created Adam and Eve, so there would have been one language from Adam to Noah, when the Flood occurred. By giving families different languages at the Tower of Babel, God was making it harder for people to get together to rebel against Him. Now because of the many languages, it is important to take the message of the gospel to people groups around the world by translating His Word into those languages.

Before the Bible was completed, God provided a special event in Jerusalem so people with different languages could hear the gospel. In Acts 2, at Pentecost, God sent the Holy Spirit to come upon the Apostles to enable them to speak in many different languages. This enabled foreign people who were there to hear the good news about Jesus.

Acts 2:1–6

23

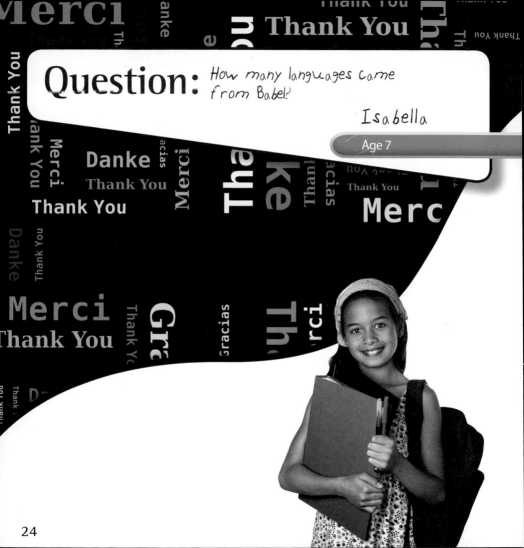

Question:

How many languages came from Babel?

Isabella

Age 7

24

Answer:

And the LORD said, "Indeed the people are one and they all have one language, and this is what they begin to do; now nothing that they propose to do will be withheld from them (Genesis 11:6).

There were at least 78 families that came out of Babel with new languages because Genesis 10 gives a listing of most of these families.

We left off Noah and his three sons since they are not listed in Genesis 10 as having been divided (Genesis 10:32). We also left off Peleg as he was probably just born or very young and kept the language of his parents, since the language division occurred "in the days of Peleg" (Genesis 10:25).

Some people in Genesis 10 were intentionally left out so that they could be discussed in Genesis 11. For example, Selah had other sons and daughters in Genesis 11:14. So that means there were a minimum of 78 language families and possibly a few more. Now these language families gave rise to almost all of the languages we have today. German, English, Norwegian, Danish, Swedish, and Austrian are all part of one language family. Latin, Italian, Spanish, French, Portuguese, and Romanian are all part of another language family. If you tally these language families up around the world, there are less than 100 language families in the world today. This is a good confirmation of what the Bible says about the origin of languages at the Tower of Babel!

Genesis 10:32; Genesis 11:13–14

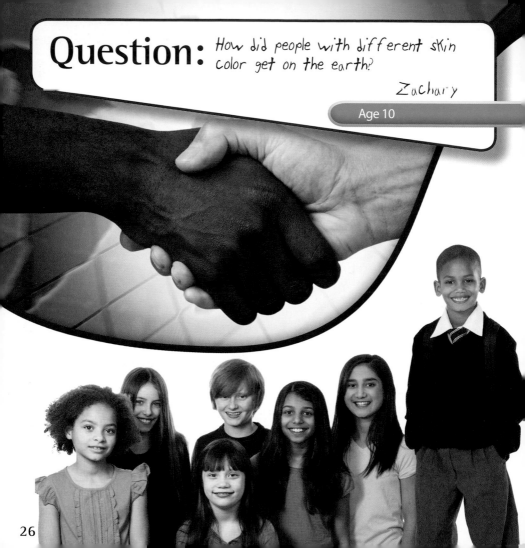

Question: How did people with different skin color get on the earth?

Zachary

Age 10

26

Answer:

Can the Ethiopian change his skin or the leopard its spots? Then may you also do good who are accustomed to do evil (Jeremiah 13:23).

Many people are under the misconception that there are different skin "colors," like red, black, white, yellow, and so on. But really, we all have the same basic skin color, from the main pigment in our skin called "melanin." This pigment is a brown color. This means that humans are all brown in color but they have different shades from dark to light.

Those people who have a lot of the brown melanin in their skin are usually called black — but they are really dark brown, not black. Those that have much less brown melanin in their skin are usually called white — but they are not white but light brown. Most people in the world are a middle brown shade. If Adam and Eve were both in the middle (middle brown) then they could have had children with dark brown skin and children with very light brown skin in one generation!

As the population split up and people left Babel by their family groups, different characteristics like the many skin shades ended up in the various groups. Some groups ended up with only dark skin, while others ended up with a light shade of skin — and others with all sorts of shades in between. What skin tone do you have?

Genesis 11:9; Acts 17:26;
John 3:16

Question: When people spread out, how did they make it to America?

Jackson

Age 9

28

Answer:

. . . and from there the LORD scattered them abroad over the face of all the earth (Genesis 11:9).

As people spread out from Babel, many of them could have walked or ridden on animals. They could easily have made it to Europe, Asia, and Africa. These continents are all connected.

But North and South America and Australia are not connected — at least not today. After the Flood, the Ice Age occurred. This event was caused by a lot of evaporation from the then-warmer oceans, and then massive snow falls on the land where it was cooler. This caused the ocean levels to be lowered by as much as 350 feet.

This would have opened up land bridges to places like North America, so that people could walk across. It also would have opened up bridges to England, Japan, and maybe even Australia. So it is possible that people and animals walked all the way to the Americas.

But let's not forget that Noah and his sons were also able to build a great ship called the ark. Many of Noah's descendants surely learned this art of shipbuilding, too. Some of Noah's descendants were even called "coastline" or "maritime" people who traveled by boat (Genesis 10:5). Many could have come to the Americas (and other places) by boats!

Genesis 6:14; Genesis 6:22;
Genesis 10:5

Question: Where did the Chinese people come from?

Ethan

Age 6

Answer:

Surely these shall come from afar; Look! Those from the north and the west, and these from the land of Sinim" (Isaiah 49:12).

All people today came out of Babel (Genesis 10:32), including the Chinese people. The Chinese came from the line of Noah's son Ham and grandson Canaan. Some of these descendants were called Canaanites. One group of Canaanites was called the Sinites (Genesis 10:15–17). Like the Sinai Peninsula, the names in the area reflect the names of Sineus or the Sinites, such as Mt. Sinai where Moses received the Ten Commandments (Exodus 34:29) when leaving Egypt.

The Chinese are descendants of these original Sinites and most call themselves "Han," from Ham, one of Noah's three sons. China in ancient times was called the land of the Sinites. This name is still used and the Bible even calls this distant land the land of Sinim (Isaiah 49:12). Not all people in China are Sinites though. There are several people groups that made it to China. One group, the Maio people, have their ancestry through Noah's son Japheth and his son Gomer. But let's remember that all people in the world are descendants of Adam — which is why all people are sinners in need of salvation through Christ.

Genesis 10:15–17; Isaiah 49:12

Question: Where do the English people come from?

Grant

Age 7

Answer:

The sons of Gomer were Ashkenaz, Riphath, and Togarmah (Genesis 10:3).

Many Americans, Australians, Canadians, and others are descendants of the English. The English live on a quite small island off the coast of mainland Europe, but they have a lot of fascinating history. Most of the English came from Germanic tribes of the northern part of mainland Europe, namely the Angles and Saxons. "Angles" is where we get the name English from (think "Anglish").

The Germanic tribes gave rise to many of the peoples of Europe, like the Swedish, Norwegians, Austrians, Germans, English, and others. The German peoples came from their ancestor Ashkenaz. Ashkenaz was the son of Gomer, the son of Japheth, the son of Noah.

Historians have a continuous record of 20 kings from King Ashkenaz until King Wolfheim Sickenger, who reigned about the same time as King Saul in Israel! Many Jews who later settled in Germanic areas like Central Europe were called "Ashkenazi Jews" and many Jews have called Germany "Ashkenaz." Some variations of the name Ashkenaz can be found in the name Scandinavia or Scandia, which is where Sweden and Norway are (think "A-scandia" or "A-scandinavia").

Jeremiah 51:27

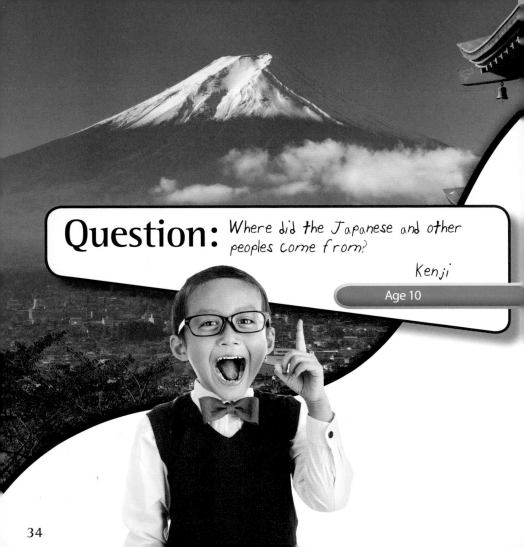

Question: Where did the Japanese and other peoples come from?

Kenji

Age 10

34

Answer:

The sons of Javan were Elishah, Tarshish, Kittim, and Dodanim (Genesis 10:4).

Many groups of people are actually descendants of more than one ancestor (although everyone is a descendant of Adam and Eve). This happened with a number of peoples, including the Japanese. A Spanish historian wrote that one of the earliest settlements on the island of Japan was by the family of Tarshish (one of Noah's great grandsons, who also inhabited one particular region of Spain), who was the son of Javan. Javan also gave rise to the Greeks, who were people who traveled by boat, so it makes sense that Tarshish would settle an island.

Several peoples invaded Japan a long time ago. Most historians think it was a mix of people from China and Mongolia. Many Japanese today are likely a mixture of some of these peoples. Here is a list of some peoples and their likely ancestry at Babel:

France: Gomer; Germany/England/Scandinavia: Ashkenaz; China: Sinites; Russia: Meshech, Tubal, Magog, Togarmah; Greece: Javan; Israelites: Arphaxad; India: Joktan, Madai, Cush; Egypt: Mizraim; Ethiopia and lower Africa: Cush. (Wow, really funny-sounding names, huh!)

Genesis 10:4–5

Question: What is the Ice Age?

Paige

Age 9

Answer:

Which are dark because of the ice, and into which the snow vanishes (Job 6:16).

The Ice Age was an event that happened after the Flood — and we believe it was generated by the Flood. At the end of the Flood, the oceans would have been warmer and the land cooler. This would have resulted in a lot of evaporation from the oceans and snow then falling on the land, resulting in a massive ice build-up on about one-third of the earth. This ice build-up would have continued for several years, causing large ice sheets and glaciers to form. Places that are naturally colder, like in the far north and the far south of earth, are the places the Ice Age affected the most. As the ice continued to build up, it pushed farther and farther into warmer areas — forming valleys.

Now evolutionary scientists think there were many ice ages over millions of years. But this isn't true. There was definitely one Ice Age several hundred years after the Flood that peaked and retreated during its duration. Since the Ice Age finally peaked, it has basically been melting and reducing ever since. But there are some places where the ice sheets are actually still growing, like in Greenland and the Antarctic Ice Cap! These places help give us an idea of what it was like when the Ice Age was growing over more of the earth.

Job 6:16–17; Job 38:22–23

Question: How does an Ice Age happen?

Obadiah

Age 6

38

Answer:

From whose womb comes the ice? And the frost of heaven, who gives it birth? (Job 38:29).

An ice age is a rare event. If the earth became very cold, it would not produce an ice age. It would just be a cold earth. For an ice age, we need warm oceans, cool land, and cool summers. With a warm ocean, this means more water would evaporate, resulting in more water in the air that would form more snow and ice, particularly in the wintertime. If there were cool summers, then all the snow and ice wouldn't melt off by the end of summer (warmer season). And with winter coming back each year, more snow and ice from each storm would make the layers of ice bigger and bigger. This is how an ice age starts.

During the Flood, several factors caused the oceans to heat up, such as the movement of the continents to their current positions. This would generate a lot of heat, just like rubbing your hands together very fast. Also high mountains and ranges formed as a result of these continental movements. When this happened, a lot of volcanoes erupted! Their eruptions shot very small ash particles into the upper atmosphere that lingered for many years. These ash particles reflected sunlight back to space and that cooled our planet down, especially in the summer. Warm oceans and cool summers are the key to an ice age. This is what would happen as a result of all the events associated with Noah's Flood.

Genesis 7:11; Psalm 104:8–9

HOLY BIBLE

Question: What was the extent of the Ice Age?

Noah

Age 10

Answer:

By the breath of God ice is given, and the broad waters are frozen (Job 37:10).

During the Ice Age, the ice extended in a downward direction from the north in Asia, Europe, and North America. It covered most of Canada, and parts of the upper United States as far down as Illinois, Indiana, and Ohio. In Europe, it extended over most of northern Europe like Sweden, Norway, and Finland, and most of England. In Asia, it covered parts of northern Russia. The ice also affected southern areas like Antarctica and stretched across the ocean almost to the southern tip of South America.

Biblical creationists (and others, even many evolutionists) agree about the extent of the ice. Where biblical creationists disagree with the secular scientists is that they think the latest ice age happened around 10,000–20,000 years ago, while we believe there was only one Ice Age and it began after the Flood, about 4,350 years ago and reached its maximum in the years following. It is possible that Job, who lived in the Middle East near the Jordan River, even saw some snow and ice that could have been associated with the time of the Ice Age. Of course, where Job lived, there was no build-up of layers into ice sheets. Most likely the snow and ice Job saw in the winter would have melted off in the summer time.

Job 6:16; Job 24:19;
Job 38:22

Question: Has anyone ever found a frozen person from the Ice Age?

Abram

Age 8

42

Answer:

"But not a hair of your head shall be lost" (Luke 21:18).

Believe it or not . . . they have found a man frozen in a glacier! He is named "Ötzi, the Iceman." His body was found frozen in ice in the Alps Mountains between Italy and Austria. The Alps Mountains in this area are specifically called the Ötztal Alps. This is why this frozen person is called Ötzi.

His body was found on September 19, 1991, by two German tourists named Helmut and Erika Simon. The body was still frozen, and part of it was hanging out of a glacier. At first, those who saw it thought it was someone who had recently died while hiking in the mountains.

But after further study, researchers realized it was a person from long ago, most likely during the Ice Age. Researchers suggest that Ötzi's body, which became mummified from the ice, is the oldest natural human mummy ever found in Europe.

He wore a cloak, coat, leggings, loincloth, and shoes. He even had a belt, a copper ax, a knife, and a quiver with 14 arrows in it! Ötzi stood about 5 feet, 5 inches tall (1.65 meters). Currently, Ötzi is on display in the South Tyrol Museum of Archaeology, which is in the farthest north province of Italy. And remember, Otzi was our relative — because he, like all people, was a descendant of Adam.

Hebrews 9:27; Ephesians 2:8

Question: How did animals make it to America and Australia after the Flood?

Walton

Age 10

44

Answer:

Bring out with you every living thing of all flesh that is with you: birds and cattle and every creeping thing that creeps on the earth, so that they may abound on the earth, and be fruitful and multiply on the earth (Genesis 8:17).

First, flying animals could make it to all sorts of places more easily than those animals that have to walk on the land. But many people instantly think land animals couldn't have walked to Australia or North and South America from the Middle East where Noah's ark landed. But we think they could have. Actually, the event of the Ice Age is very important here. During the Ice Age, a lot of water was taken out of the oceans and accumulated on the land in the form of ice and snow. Most think that the ocean level dropped by about 350 feet! This drop would expose land bridges in different places throughout the world. Remember that Noah and his sons built the ark and it survived a global Flood! Noah lived 350 years after the Flood and Shem lived 500 years after it too. So they could easily have shared how to build some pretty neat ships. Many people could have traveled by boat to the Americas, Australia, Madagascar, and other places, possibly taking animals with them.

It makes you wonder how many animals have been taken to various parts of the world by people and we just don't have a record of it.

Genesis 9:28; Genesis 11:10–11;
Genesis 10:5

45

Question: What Kinds of animals lived in the areas affected by the Ice Age?

Eve, Jackson, and Zachary

Ages 8, 9, & 7

46

Answer:

A righteous man regards the life of his animal, but the tender mercies of the wicked are cruel (Proverbs 12:10).

The animals that lived during the Ice Age, specifically in the icy areas or more properly the areas between the ice, would be the animals that were well-equipped to handle the cold (think of furry animals) and still find food. These animals were primarily warm-blooded mammals. There were many animals that would do well, but the more famous ones were the saber-toothed cat, woolly mammoth, dire wolf, giant beaver, snowshoe hare (rabbit), mastodon, short-faced bear, musk ox, and many others like types of shrews, moles, and skunks.

Many of these have gone extinct since the Ice Age, like the saber-toothed cats, dire wolves, mastodons, and mammoths. But some have survived, like the snowshoe hares, arctic shrews, and star-nosed moles found in Minnesota and Wisconsin. At the Creation Museum, we have a replica of the third-largest and most complete skeleton of a mastodon ever found. It has flint markings on its ribs from spears and arrowheads, which help us understand that hunters were able to kill this massive creature. Man was not allowed to eat meat until after the Flood, and the Ice Age occurred after the Flood.

Genesis 1:29; Genesis 9:3;
Mark 7:19

47

Answers Are Always Important!

The Bible is truly filled some amazing answers for some of our toughest faith questions. If you would like to know more about how the sons and grandsons of Noah are at the heart of man's earliest history. Now trace your cultural history back to survivors of the Great Flood:

www.answersingenesis.org/assets/pdf/2013/chart-of-people-groups.pdf

The Answers Book for Kids series answers questions from children around the world in this multi-volume series. Each volume will answer over 20 questions in a friendly and readable style appropriate for children 6–12 years old; and each covers a unique topic including, Creation and the Fall; Dinosaurs and the Flood of Noah; God and the Bible; and Sin, Salvation, and the Christian Life, and more!